I0450066

Adam's Rib
An Invitation To Reality

by
Meir Naman

authorHOUSE™

1663 LIBERTY DRIVE, SUITE 200
BLOOMINGTON, INDIANA 47403
(800) 839-8640
WWW.AUTHORHOUSE.COM

First published by AuthorHouse 07/22/05

ISBN: 1-4208-6133-6 (sc)

Library of Congress Control Number: 2005904880

Printed in the United States of America
Bloomington, Indiana

This book is printed on acid-free paper.

It was 1979, we had made it to L.A. the air here is different, all my friends were here. It was summer and I was eleven. My friends consisted of two cousins and my brother of fourteen, among others. All my family was here except for my parents. They had remained behind to salvage what was left of our wealth. My father had done well in his life and looming was the thoughts of late action. We lived the four of us in a two bedroom apartment; second floor. My sister, two brothers, and I. Living arrangements were less luxurious here. We had to clean. I was under the care of my sister of eighteen and my brother of twenty one. We got along.

Those early summer days we spent at the park and the arcade. The lack of luxury was compensated by abundance in availability. I was excited for having made it out. That was when my mother who had brought me here returned to be with my father. My father continued his craft back home. Soon came September and I was enrolled in school. That two bedroom apartment was leased, because it was across the street from the school.

The neighborhood was safe. Seventh grade, one day they took me there and I stayed. Mrs Smith, ESL. The language barrier was enormous. I did not speak the language and I did not know the school. Those who tried to befriend me I was too shy to indulge, and those who had been influenced by the news were unkind and seemed to be the majority. The news was of the hostage crisis, count of days was the backdrop of every newscast, Jimmy Carter was president . Those early days were tough. Yet I was oblivious and spirited.

My new friends in school consisted of those who were in the same predicament. The teachers were all kind, and soon I learned the language and life became routine. I was always younger than all my friends. I was also the younger of my cousins too. My built small, I was the bullies pick. What complicated matters was that I was nice and resilient. Although I didn't like it I did not cower. I have been a late bloomer all my life. Oh the liberties that some children take. In High School I withdrew from socializing; yet, I still sought the places that those whom I could not socialize with, bragged about. The circle of squares, only we didn't even make a circle. The places proved boring and the lifestyle wasteful.

My sense of a lack of fulfilment in my social life, lead to my interest in learning to play guitar. The music of this land proved comforting and my interest in music seemed natural. Rock and Roll had matured in the seventies. The songs offered much in life experience. There, was the attraction; the talk of city life. Quickly though, New Wave emerged on to the scene and, almost over night Rock and Roll was over shadowed by Pop music. I remained in the interest of discovering Rock and Roll. This caused further drift between my contemporaries and myself. I found myself more and more isolated. Yet, the evolution in my musical development offered enough satisfaction to compensate. Later I learned that lyrics offer structure to a song; and thereby, began to sing and to write songs. Every song causes joy when written and also when put to music . Oh the splendor of private fulfilment. The joy remains at the occasion of every harmonized revisitation.

Those were the days of braces and part time cashiering at the fast food joint. The days of dance clubs on Saturday nights. Feelings of inadequacy. The desire to know women. Being rude to teachers. Bicycles, and bus passes. Beach and basketball. Oh and the guitar.

My father arrived in L.A. in 1981. His attempts of salvaging his wealth had failed. As such, he had come into close encounters with the governing entity, which confiscated most of his assets. Dismayed and tired he showed up and spent some time without work. Devestated he was; and in longing for my mother who had stayed behind. My mother made it out and came to L.A. in 1983. What a joy it was to see her, she cried at the airport. Soon after my sister got married and moved away. Separation from dear ones is difficult, yet often it allows for pleasant visitation. During those years of separation from my mother, my sister took it upon herself to care for me. She cared for all of us. The sense of generosity that I feel today, and my moral discipline, have been cultivated by my sister to this day.

By the time highschool was over, my father had rallied my two brothers into starting the business; and, as I started my freshman year of college I had a new job as part time secretary. The office was six hundred square feet in downtown, on 9th street, 4th floor. It consisted of the office and the lunch room. Three days of work, two days of school. We were in the electronics wholesale market; which later lead to importation. In the early days there was still room for domestic trade. Later, we found further demand within the export markets. So years later, I was in the Import/Export business.

The university was better, even from the start. No roll call. Didn't need a note to be absent. In highschool we had an attendance office that kept all the notes on file. This was like Disnyland. Coffee and Tobacco. The cafeteria had a smoking section. We would schedule classes to maximize time in the cafeteria. Early on, I took a liking towards economics for my major. It proved to be of enourmous benefit. A gem of a science. The study of the way things are. Of course with emphasis on our modern age. There were no thoughts of post graduate study. I attended only the classes which interested me, and crammed for the rest. I got by fine. A "C" was good enough for me. Oh the fun times. I finished with a "B" Average. I was a natural.

It was junior year, I had been accepted to UCLA. I had seen her a few times before in the study hall. Now, we were sharing the corner table in the Downstairs study hall. Conversation was smooth. I was shy. After a few months we were going steady. She was beautiful. High pitched voice, and a youthful disposition. Me the ever late bloomer. We got along grand. We were the best of friends. We were both about twenty, she a year older. The relation ship lasted about a year. I learned about my jealous side. But only of its existence. I was without any understanding of what it is and how to control it. On the other hand my jealousy seemed to have complete control over my behavior. Oh the shame I felt for having treated her with such disrespect. We were young, both inexperienced. But as in all the other cases that came up; I was the culprit. Later on, I turned the volume so high that nothing would even happen. I would offend them very subtly right from the start, so they knew to stay away. I didn't do this consciously. It seems that once I was aware of the existence of my jealous side; I didn't try to control it, and so was able to observe it. But I became aware of this only years later. A jealous man feels cut when his jealousy is exposed by a woman; however, those feelings afford room for further growth, even beyond the so called "growing ages". "It takes two to tango."

By the end of my senior year, I had so much material written over the break up, that all of a sudden I had a repertoire. It took six months. I was devestated. It was first love. It took me years to recover fully. If there is such a thing? Any way, at the time I became friends with a classmate who was in the same predicament. Only, he had a younger sister. Oh what a joy she was. A smile on her face at all times. Intelligent. Wise. Loyal. My only contact with her was as a friend of her brother's. She never consented to anything more.

Soon I was infatuated with her. In all fairness I let her brother know. He did not object. So I would call her in the afternoons.

By now I was already in the business full time. I had graduated and was in awe of the mannerisms in the way merchants communicate with each other. Much goes on in the confines of commerce as it stretches along the fabric of our lives. Soon I became as they were and learned the names and learned the tasks. The business world proved rewarding. There is no regulation in the rate of learning as in school, and there is much to learn. Those phone calls in the afternoon were a break in the action. But I looked forward to them. She was so delightful. Yet all that changed when I told her of my infatuation with her. I think I might have used the word love. She did not consent. She took my phone calls after that, but the sweetness was now guarded.

It was my understanding of song writing, and her generosity that allowed for this friendship to continue. As sporadic as communication took place through the years, she was in my thoughts. When we spoke she exposed my weaknesses; and in time, I became strong. Longing for someone does provide for moments of inspiration; and, inspiration is a necessary element of any craft. I found myself being disciplined by a very disciplined individual, which was rewarding enough. The songs were an added advantage. Whether in pleasure or perceived pain, moments of learning justify the passage of time. The culmination of learning into craft is art and cause for celebration.

By the time my encounter with the angel of kindness was bestowed upon me, I was about thirty. She was twenty seven. Of her I learned kindness towards another. I did consider myself nice, and that must have been my merit. Here was confirmation that my search for unconditional love had not been in vain. As always the learning was not automatic, and much of the conclusions were made upon retrospect. At the time that it happened; it was sheer bliss. The form that the learning took was the realization that I was not nice at all. I was allowed to measure myself against her kindness and I seized the opportunity. Shedding the layers of illusion seem to be the most difficult task of all. Women, properly understood are able to point the way; and as such, are a necessary component. The task however; is dependant on the inspired enthusiasm, active participation, and the perseverance of man.

She was aware of herself, her likes and dislikes. Always in good spirit. For that time I felt loved. Of course getting over that did not prove pleasant. This wasn't a break up. This was a parting of two people of integrity. A sweet farewell, in words of praise and prayers of blessed paths ahead. It has remained a learning experience of great worth; and somehow we knew it will be that, all along the way. Now the day had come, as I had promised her. I was alone, and I had been set upon a path, and there was no turning back. My greed was shrinking day by day. I now noticed my difficulty to relate. I became a home body. Being kind in an unkind world?

Her influence was the source of my pleasure; it was the realities of commerce and culture which now were the sources of my displeasure. More so, by now I had already become comfortable in both fields, and remained welcome in both by my peers and associates. Yet, I have always known, that when fate calls there is no other option but to heed the call. And as slow as progress took, there was no turning back.

2. The Garden

The garden is where I grew up. It was grounds to three houses. My father's, my uncle's, and my grandfather's. Fruit and berry trees, vegetable gardens, a pool for each house, apple orchard, a well, hens and roosters, turkeys and ducks, pigeons and dogs, and open spaces separated by Elm, Pine, and Sycamore trees. The whole garden was surrounded by walls, and outside was the sidewalk. They had purchased a large plot of land in the outskirts. Later the city grew in that direction, and the neighborhood became a residential suburb. Values increased substantially. So they built and moved in. The garden was cultivated by my uncle and my father. By the time I was born they had just moved in. I am the youngest of the grand children, on my father's side. By age eleven, the revolution forced us out that was 1979. The contrast in living arrangements was enourmous. The garden had provided me the freedom to roam in security without the need for a chaperone. Instead of Those large rooms and hallways, we were now living in a two bedroom apartment in Beverly Hills.

My sentiments about the garden have been grand through out. I continually feel the benefit of having had such a large space around me as a child. It has been a source of serenity, and allowed for the development of my thought processes. Oh the glorious walks, the blessed soil. A paradise. Often I reminisce.

The revolution was the first real encounter I had with my minority status in a predominantly Moslem country. Decedents of Israel, we were a small minority community in Tehran. My exposure to this community had been limited to extended family, and temple on holidays. As a child I had been told about the days of my grand father's youth when this community was restricted to a ghetto existence. Now there was fear in our hearts. The news was of great importance. After the revolution, there was news of the execution of prominent members of this same community. The level of fear was enourmous. Later my father opted to leave every thing behind. Many of the same community fled to L.A. and other parts of the world.

At that time, the most tangible form in which I felt this experience, was that I had lost my paradise. I decided that I would not miss it; rather, I would be grateful for having had it. This did allow for pure enjoyment of fond memories, especially during those awkward years of adolescence. Also the experience, and my childhood, remain purely as sources of inspiration. The one time that I heard that it had dried up for not having been tended to; I was upset for a while. That was around the time my uncle passed away. Now I hear there's some government office working out of our home back in Tehran. I always hope that the garden is still there and those old trees are still alive. The memories fade as time goes by, but the lessons remain. This one has served me well through the years and remains.

3. The Cultural Balance

I was born at a time in Iran's history, when for two generations the kingdom had been ruled by the institution of secular laws. This after centuries of religious laws. The difference had been a more protective and welcoming environment for the minority groups in the land, whereas the religious influence had been oppressive and exclusive. The result had been unsurpassed growth and prosperity within the relatively new secular society. Civil laws had replaced religious laws, opening opportunity to women and minority groups. The revolution, again caused an abrupt return to the religious laws, as opposed to the civil laws. yet I didn't experience that first hand.

What I experienced was a culture shock. For the American public, the most tangible experience of the revolution was the hostage crisis of the early eighties. As horrendous as it was; in school the children did not understand that the new immigrants are also victims of this same event. This caused separation. It is interesting that now, I was being treated rudely but for entirely different reasons. This time it was my nationality and not my heritage. Fortunately, the treatment was only among the peers, and not among the establishment; which did allow me inclusion in commendable form. What was lacking in the interaction with my peers was fulfilled by music, movies, and the media. My friendships were formed within the community of immigrants for the most part.

What is interesting in learning different cultures intricately, is that dichotomies are created in the personality. I found that Farsi, English, and a mixture of both; are each a different mode of my personality; such that, I can only function in one at a time, and my personality is different in each mode. The key in learning any culture is to learn the language. Learning a language is much easier when approached from a cultural perspective. Ultimately, the cultural perspective is a necessary component in learning any dialect fully. These simple realities were only clear to me as a result of having the opportunity to learn the Spanish language, via the Latin American dialects, mostly by exposure to the Mexican culture.

By the end of my college years, I had already assimilated in good form within the United States. My first romance, which was during my junior year, did also provide me with some further and welcomed exposure to the American culture. This is when, having already created a following for our products; we started to see customers coming up from Mexico, looking for our location. In the good spirit of commerce we welcomed them. They didn't speak English, and we didn't speak any Spanish. As their demand for product increased so did our interaction, and I started to pick up the language. Before long, I was traveling regularly to Mexico and other Latin American countries. Most of my interactions were taking place in the Spanish language. Having already experienced the benefits of learning the American culture. I embraced the opportunity to learn the Mexican culture as best as I could. Native American presence and cultural influence are far more apparent and integrated within the Latin and the South Americas, than in the USA.

The most enlightening lesson, that my friend's younger sister taught me, took form over a single phone conversation. After having spoken some kind words to me on the phone just a few days before. Here I was pressing the issue, for her to arrive at some confession of fondness towards me. As she refused, I became anxious and confronted her by asking her; "didn't you say those things the last time we spoke"? To which she replied; "yes but that's changing by the second." What can I say, I was stopped in my tracks. I was behaving rudely. She was right as usual.

In the Mexican culture the concept of a "man's word" takes an entirely different form. There exists much more understanding towards the fact; that people have the right to change their mind without notice. Insistence, though unlikely, might occur over important issues. Judgement however, is nonexistent.

They say that one cannot teach an old dog new tricks. It took me a long time to accept that people really do have the right to change their mind, and there's nothing I can do about that. As I became more practiced, I did realize that with such understanding, I experience disappointment far less frequently. Relaxation became a far more tangible concept, and my attitude is far more personable. I would never be the same again. I had always believed that my word is my bond. Now I had learned to really prioritize that concept, and let go of the unimportant stuff. Only then realizing, that there is far more unimportant issues than important issues. And, if the important issues are not to one's satisfaction; then maybe one should look elsewhere, instead of talking about it. Of course, with the exception of immediate family.

The Persian culture is refined in the art of hospitality. This seemingly the influence of its Zoroastrian heritage. The Farsi language is rich and powerfully versatile. Expressions of love, selflessness, forgiveness, mysticism, and enlightenment; have been captured masterfully in the poetry of the culture. During periods of repressive rulership, the same is accomplished in very subtle forms, for which in-depth knowledge of the language is required. Yet, they stand as a testament to the level of refinement in politeness, which gives this culture such grace in hospitality.

In the Persian culture, although benevolence towards all is of noble value, in being a host to a welcomed guest, pride is enjoyed in the level of consideration, afforded the guest. Appropriate comfort of guests in their enjoyment, and their fondness of the encounter being the measure. As such the people of this culture have become so refined in the art, that they usually make very kind and considerate guests.

As a point of comparison, the Farsi language contains two distinct forms of address in the formal and the informal language. For example, the second person singular pronouns are not the same in the formal and the informal language. This being also a characteristic of the Spanish language as well. Yet in the English language this is not the case. In the English language the second person pronoun is the same whether singular or plural; formal or informal. Seemingly this is a point of no consequence. Yet the ability to express respect and to establish hierarchies is greatly facilitated in the former; manifesting refinement in consideration and, politeness towards others. And taken in good time refinement can be an ever continuing process. This is especially apparent in the Persian culture, given its age dating back to the ancient times.

At the time that I was learning to speak the Spanish language, this simple grammatical similarity proved very useful in acquiring encouraging and patient guidance from my counterparts, for which I remain grateful. Whether manifest or coincidental, the American culture seems to be much less considerate of hierarchical considerations; which affords its own delights that do come to light, especially when afforded a point of comparison. These delights, seem to take form in removing perceived limits of the imagination; facilitating the evolution and the realization of thought, in any chosen field. The integration of the two concepts has been a difficult yet fruitful endeavor, with potential for continued refinement.

The Hebrew culture is another part of this great balancing act. Unity, and the confirmation of hierarchy, are effectively maintained in the Hebrew culture. Great emphasis is placed on family relations, as is prescribed by the good book; which does establish the existence of hierarchical boundaries among family members. As such, this does extend to the extended family and the larger community in the form of respect for elders. Consequently, great importance is placed on parenting, causing great affect towards immediate family. Although these characteristics are apparent in all other cultures as well; here, they have been commanded in good form to begin with, and seem to have been further fortified by the historical treatment of this race by the nations of the world.

It also seems, that the criteria for teaching these traits to the children is any means possible, and as long as it takes. As such, the use of guilt and insistence although not so comforting, are allowed. The result is a deep sense of affection towards fellow Israelites, and the culture itself; or unity. And looming always is the fear of social discrimination and persecution. It seems that there are many similarities between the Hebrew culture and the African-American culture. Both coming from a history of slavery, and both still subject to some level of social discrimination. Also it seems that neither race is fully aware of these cultural similarities, and their potential for mutual growth and friendship. The differences seem to exist in the ages of the two cultures.

The balancing act proved exhausting; yet, the efforts did leave enough behind to allow me to recuperate and to incorporate the lessons gathered, as the task continues to date. Today, I feel more lost than I ever have in my life, yet I still know that its not true.

4. Commerce

Commerce proved to be the source of yet another dichotomy in my character. Here, was exposure to numerous other cultures, including the far east countries; yet, the commercial task itself is blind to cultural distinctions. I often would think that some of the nicest social visits would occur over business. This is true because usually the cause of visitation is some commercial necessity, which bears the burden for the encounter; leaving the parties to participate at will in brief impartation, before attending to the matter of interest. As for those matters of interest; they are measurable only in numbers, according to generally accepted principals, regardless of who is attending to them.

Trust seems to be the necessary element in commerce; because, transaction costs increase greatly in the absence of trust, making it impossible to compete on a continuous basis. This is set in an environment where many abuse the trust which has been endowed. So the object is to choose counterparts of trustworthy integrity, and to limit the level of exposure, at the same time. Of course, one has to be of trustworthy integrity to begin with. After all, good faith remains as the only source of true profit in the long run; and, even that is not entirely immune to the elements, or the times.

As always, common respect is also necessary and facilitated by the mechanical nature of the task. However, ultimately it is not attainable without the existence of self respect. It is not the case that these principals are of value only in commerce; yet, the arena does provide an environment, where these principals are more practically comprehendible. the experiences and their lessons are applicable to all parts of life.

A note on hard work. It is also necessary. Objectivity is key in that one should strive to provide what is needed; which is defined by the task at hand and not the individual. Efficiency, aims to minimize disruptions to flow, diminishing necessity for interference, without compromising integrity. Much pressure is brought to bear on people in the business world. A balance must arise; because, besides the day to day, one must also work hard at maintaining patience, integrity, courage, compassion, flexibility, humility, and readiness. Many times, the best course of action is to wait. On the other hand, opportunities can fade quickly if not seized. It is hard work to learn the difference. Commerce occurs on a continuous basis. One should take pace.

My father had been a successful businessman, for the greater part of his life. Now in times of great change in our lives, he had brought us together to start building again. In the process he would endow us with all of his wisdom. The very commendable attitude which he displayed, was taking a consulting role; leaving all active negotiations, decision making and implementations, up to his sons. Letting us learn by experience in a controlled format.

It was my role as the training supervisor for the hired staff, which I enjoyed the most. Early on, we had learned that hiring relatively inexperienced individuals, and teaching them the job was more cost effective; considering that anyone we hired, would need some training. The positions were; dispatcher, bookkeeper and receptionist. The departments; traffic, accounting, and administration.

Teaching is rewarding in a more immediate manner, as well as long term. Ultimately, teaching is the catalyst for learning. The common idea imparted in each position, was that of self respect. In a business format, this took shape in getting them to understand that they have the right to know what is expected of them. If they are unclear, they have the right to ask. The repetitive nature of the job, and the need to do it correctly. That they should not be pushed around by anyone. That they have the right to refuse. And, that in an organization of trustworthy integrity; all are working towards common good, along with the larger business community. The aim was to give them a sense of responsibility, so that they could enjoy the freedoms that come with that. Namely, less encounters with the supervisor. Watching them was easy. It is true that numbers never lie. For those who would stay, soon we would have very confident and respectable individuals working among us. There is immense pride involved, with witnessing a scared individual transform into a confident one; having provided the environment for that to occur. Also, understanding that what they have learned will remain with them, in other parts of their lives as well.

As for me, I learned a great deal. This is one that only can be understood by experience. One needs to actively teach, in order to understand how it is a catalyst for learning. One guideline, is that care should be taken to impart with information that has only benefitted the teacher, and no part should be left out . Only in an advisory position one could impart information that has caused negative or fearful effects in his own mind, and only to warn a fellow of the pitfalls of such ideas, and usually only if solicited. There is great responsibility in teaching, while advice should always contain a disclaimer. Where is the line? Much refinement of character can occur in attempting to find an honest answer. The number of things to share diminishes greatly, and one can live by one's own example. Realizing that life is a unique experience for every individual, and that people are, and should be free, to be who they are. Consequences of actions are only part of that freedom and do not void the freedom itself. What is common to all these individual experiences, is where the line is. Only through teaching the good fully, objectively, and without reservation, can one love another as oneself. One note of self respect; if you have nothing nice to say it is perfectly alright if you should choose to not say anything at all.

It was in those years after the university years, that I came to feel betrayed by the notion that I had been taught, in my biology classes. The notion being that "human beings are a product of genetics and their environment." Understanding the level of the generality of the statement, and also the empirical nature of the science, I don't feel betrayed anymore. However, the feelings took shape; because of the lack of emphasis on the necessity of the individual's choice, in forming their own character. In time, one can become whoever one wills to be, and human will can only be focused by the individuals choosing. I had only begun to realize the necessity of analyzing and formulating ideas, and deciding where I stood on my own issues. To sort out the baggage of information I had been provided with. What is of key interest, is that this is a time consuming process. In order for one to make an intelligent choice about any issue of one's own choosing; it is necessary for one to review and ponder the criteria surrounding the issue at hand, and then to consciously make a choice. Since this is to occur in the solitude of the mind; many times, the option of choice is not even recognized. Ultimately, it is true that one chooses according to one's own preferences. However it is of utter importance for one to be well aware of those preferences, as well as one's priorities, knowing that they can change with the passing of time.

Another point of interest, which follows from the same line of thinking, is that human beings more than anything need to feel a sense of worth. This idea, although commonly overlooked, is true because without this sense of worthiness, existence becomes burdensome. Although commonly overlooked, this idea is central to the trade of motivational writing or speaking. Given an environment where one can allow another a sincere sense of self worth, though limited in scope, can afford much blessing for all involved, in the totality of their lives. Yet one does not need look far for the opportunity; for even as we breath, our kinsmen are before us, and the larger community as well. Only the development of an objective and sincere awareness, in the manner in which one relates to all things, is necessary. This although difficult to grasp at first, in time can take place naturally. Given that the realm of learning contains enough worth for all, it is possible that two or more individuals can afford each other the same sense of worth, simultaneously. This is the old "win / win" scenario. It is always available as the best option in any situation; however, It will not work if attempted with insincerity. Most important, is to understand that people are allowed to make mistakes. Respect when offered freely and without expectations, usually goes a long way. Remember, that the first rule of respect is self respect. Also, a sense of humor can help greatly as always. And if anyone thinks that he or she does not have a sense of humor, it is only because he or she is not aware of its existence at that time.

What remains is memories, and many more that have been forgotten. Many friends in distant parts. The opportunity to continue on to a different field of business. Commerce, with all of its pitfalls, does remain as the best way to experience the larger community. For that I remain grateful. For it is by the perspective of another, that one can ponder self and fashion it according to one's own choosing. Life has had a way of carrying me away. I also have a way of getting carried away. It's been like that since childhood. No sense in complaining. Uncertainty can be exhilarating at times.

5. Hebrew Philosophy

I had already been working for a few years out of college, when out of my need for some moral clarity, I referred myself to the old book of our good faith. It was my father's Torah. I had too many questions. It was at that same time when I was figuring things out. My upbringing was now face to face with the outside world. There was such a large difference between the two. Old friendships did not feel the same anymore. Everyone including myself was busy doing something, and being carried by life in a different direction. There was room only for romance, and that was non existent at the time. Only infatuation. Also after college the frequency of my song writing diminished greatly; however when I wrote, the quality was better because I was pondering more and seldom dreamed.

Hebrew philosophy today, remains as the most influential philosophy in our world. It is out of this philosophy, that modern; Judaism, Christianity and Islam, have taken form as religions. It is also one of the most accessible philosophies; as the writings remain among the most widely translated and distributed in the world. The Torah consists of the first five books in the Holy Bible: Genesis, Exodus, Leviticus, Numbers, and Deuteronomy. The entire remainder of what is known as the "Old Testament," consists of a collection of ancient Hebrew writings, which have remained over the years; each marking a different period in the history of the nation. Spanning the centuries from the time of the crossing of the Jordan river, up to the birth of the Savior. From a philosophical stand point, it remains true that the ancient Israelites did feel a stronger need than their contemporaries, to record their own history. With the addition of the new testament, which is another collection of writings marking the periods after the birth of the Savior, the Holy Bible is formed.

The significant distinguishing factor in Hebrew philosophy, is the emphasis on the Torah, as a separate and complete book. The remainder of the books which make up the Holy Bible take form as sources of history, prophecy, and testimony to the Torah. Although they impart moral and inspirational guidance, they serve as signposts guiding their reader to the Torah; which is the source of the teachings. However, only the reading of the Torah is necessary in understanding the Hebrew philosophy and Judaism as a faith, in their entirety. The remainder of the canonized writings, remain available for further academic endeavors; whether inspirational, historical, or prophetical.

As such, according to Hebrew philosophy, the Torah remains as the only instrument for divine wisdom and guidance in this world. What is commonly referred to as; "The Word of God" or "The Good Book". In this light, the Torah is deemed complete and entirely perfect, in bringing about the necessary understanding of the different facets of life, for anyone who reads it. The Israelites are deemed merely, as the race which God chose to make an example of, before the nations of our world. As such, much wisdom is imparted in the account of their interactions with God, during their migration from Egypt to the Promised Land. The same is true of the accounts, of the interactions of God with the various individuals, which appear in the book of Genesis. Also specific guidance is provided for day to day matters and social order, as in the book of Leviticus.

It was with this understanding that I undertook my search for moral clarity. My aim was to understand the logic behind all the do's and don'ts which I had been raised with. As such, my endeavor did not extend beyond the book of Deuteronomy.

What I learned, is that the accounts of the various individuals' experiences with God, each bear various lessons to be learned from. For example I will list some. Adam and Eve, exemplify the differences between men and women and between humans and God. Cane and Able, impart a lesson in jealousy. Noah, a lesson in common decency. Abraham, a lesson in faith. Isaac, a lesson in order. Jacob, a lesson in fate. Joseph, a lesson in forgiveness. Moses, a lesson in strength. The Israelites, a lesson in God's forgiving nature. Aside from these examples, the accounts bear literally countless other lessons, which become even clearer upon occasional revisitation. The very interesting concept remains, that although these various qualities are each exemplified within different accounts and individuals; the reader can incorporate all within one individual. Absorb the good and become aware of the bad. In this way, a solid foundation is provided to build upon.

The fundamental aim of Hebrew philosophy seems to be; to dissuade the reader from the act of idolatry. The effect of idolatry, over time, is a state of perpetual fear. Essentially, idolatry is born out of a state of perpetual fear. The removal of idolatry from any individual's belief system, is not possible without providing a replacement, to neutralize the state that existed, before the practice began. Here, although the reader is specifically instructed that; God may not be found in anything which takes physical form. A clear and highly informative code; of conduct and social order, is provided as testimony to Gods existence and the way to understand God. As such, the Torah is so effective in achieving this aim, that over time, the reader is dissuaded from any form of superstitious thinking. Because all forms of superstitious thinking involve some form of charm or talisman. Although during the transition period, one requires the reliance on God to overcome one's fears; the end result is that over time, self reliance is learned; such that, the reader no longer requires reliance on God; and , fear is transformed to Love. Distinction is made between God and God's creation, and the function of each as God intends.

On a personal note. I have learned that today, my knowledge of "what God is"; exists only to the extent of my love for God, and my knowledge of "what God is not". Understanding also, that my beloved is the Creator, referred to in the Torah; and, that my love has grown out of the understanding of life, which God has endowed to me, by way of the Torah. This love is inclusive of the creation as well, for it is my beloved's creation, and myself only a part thereof. These understandings were not clear to me initially after having read the Torah. However, it seemed that immediately and automatically; a process of deliberation had begun within my mind. Over the years as I have been able to apply the lessons which I have learned to my experiences; this deliberation process has evolved, and continues to grow with the passing of time.

Another distinct characteristic of Hebrew philosophy, is the criteria of inclusion. Being patriarchal in nature, and particular about lineage; the criteria of inclusion is: To be born to an Israelite man regardless of the mother's race. Accordingly, with respect to women, marriage to an Israelite constitutes inclusion as well. The maintaining and teaching of moral order within a family, is deemed primarily the responsibility of man. This responsibility being rooted in objective fairness, rather than commanding authority; the latter not being possible without the existence of the former. It should also be noted that within the Israelites, circumcision seems to be the only criteria of inclusion within the covenants made between God and The patriarchs; namely Abraham, Isaac, and Jacob. Inclusion however, is not a condition for anyone to read the examples that God has set in the Torah, and to learn there from.

Final point of interest, is that in Hebrew philosophy the concept of an "after-life" or "life after death" is not addressed. Whether such realities exist or not is not made to be of concern for the reader. Aside from history and lineage, the Torah only imparts wisdom for better lives. The concepts of "hell" and "the devil" seem to have found their way into world philosophies, from other sources. Yet, they are completely incompatible with the concept of one God, as proclaimed in the Torah.

Needless to say, that my endeavor in gaining a sense of moral clarity, proved to be much more fruitful than I expected. The experience remains as the most significant part of my life. Life is full of wonder. It seems that people can either be looking for God, and getting confused in the process; or, they can behold Gods creation and ultimately, recognize God's light reflecting. Before one can do the latter; one would need to know the difference between God, and God's Creation.

6. The Dance of Gender

Given the premise that gentleness is a function of strength; as opposed to fragility being a function of weakness.   At least in modern urban culture, It remains a fallacy popular among men, the notion that "women in general are impossible to understand." This not referring to language; rather, to their mannerisms and ways as they differ with the mannerisms and ways common to men.   The ways of nature are not so.   Nature in essence, works under full disclosure terms.   One only need make the necessary inferences, to understand that which beguiles them.   True, that coming into the picture without knowledge, and being provided with a historical perspective by way of expectation; this ability to make inferences should take some time to develop.   Yet this is a path in which any advancement is nonretractable, neither even by the will of the traveler.   The very technology that we enjoy in our present age is a product of generations of such endeavors of discovery, yet in the fields of mechanics. All necessary and fundamental discoveries have been learned through inferences from nature.   Certainly any individual can practice the same in application to their own private life and mind as well.

Another commonly popular fallacy that exists mostly among women, at least in modern urban culture; is the notion that "most men look for their mother when seeking a mate". The inference being to one who bares the qualities which the man's mother contains. The truth is that the face of humanity is at least, as diverse as the number of people who inhabit this earth. In most modern cultures however the decision of choosing a mate is usually limited to only one, out of this multitude of diversity. The same being necessary of both individuals simultaneously.

The single distinguishing factor universal to both genders is their role in the reproductive process, and the physical attributes of this reality. They are not distinguishable however in their interdependence on one another. Only together; they can achieve a state that once obtained is not retractable. the state of parenthood. It seems however, that the role that women assume in bearing and suckling the conceived, has much to do with the existence of what is commonly referred to as "Women's intuition." True kindness and loyalty, although instinctively endowed to women by the mothering instinct, seem to be more illusive, and remain as things to learn; for men. The distinction is that because of their instinctive nature, these traits are not readily available if the woman is in a defensive frame of mind. Yet these qualities are not restricted only to the child; rather, they permeate all of womanhood and are readily available to those worthy. What complicates the matter, is that humanity remains guilty of a history of disrespect towards women; and, there could be no other culprit but us men. Somehow a patriarchal form of maintaining lineage, has transformed into dominance due to superior physical strength.

The truth is that one has been used as an excuse for the other. Through the generations, this has taken a form of instinctive and subtle disregard for women by men. Although in many cultures it is still at the stage of oppression. Even in this modern age, and even if the basics of respect are provided; inclusion is not. In the American culture inclusion is further protected by way of labeling, men who are considerate of women, as "sissies". The very necessity and the existence of what is known as the "feminist movement" is testimony to this reality. The unfortunate result is that today, most women spend far more time and effort protecting their integrity, than they do being intuitive. However, the intuition is always available in an environment of integrity. This, Although remains known to most men in their private lives; somehow changes as it approaches the social arena. Yet if any part of any whole is incomplete then the whole is incomplete as well. It seems that men have systematically and effectively deprived themselves, and their counterparts, of the learning that would bring them that peace which they so crave. Logic would dictate that the physical strength of man would increase enormously, if he were to choose to not assume an oppressive reality; because, he would have an ally instead of a dependant as a mate?

To men is endowed scope. That is the ability to take simple concepts and apply them in large scale. To women is endowed vision, through the understanding of life's changing nature. To clarify further, women are generally more considerate of feelings and emotions whereas men are generally more considerate of accomplishments.

There in is the dance of gender. Where each respective quality is available to the other through learning and refinement. With this perspective; any willful encounter with members of the opposite sex, can be a learning experience; given common respect and fearless communication. Further, it remains that the level of the maturity of any individual; is a function of the level of one's understanding of the opposite sex as well as one's own and the differences between the two. This understanding can provide much serenity in life. As in all learning; the desire and willingness of the learner necessary.

What is being recommended here is the understanding that one does not need to know the entire population of the other gender, to gain an understanding of the opposite sex. Yet, it is in the actual encounters that one does have, whether intimate, familial, or social; that one can apply oneself in learning an understanding of the opposite sex over an extended period of time, that being however long it takes in each individual case. What distinguishes discipline; is worth, and consistency over time. It might be deemed dismissive to declare the task impossible to begin with, especially with the availability of historical perspective. In this light trust would not be able to flourish, therefore obliterating the prospect from the start, leaving us exactly where we remain; rightfully mistrustful and busy protecting our integrity. Catch 22.

The flip side of this idea, is the law of pressure which states that; 'any entity applying any form of pressure upon another, is also subjected to that same amount of pressure for the entire duration that the pressure continues.' A word of insight; if you are applying the pressure and your counter part is a roach, it would cease. Yet, when your counterpart is human, with a cosmic mind; the continuation of pressure, no matter how small, can ware on both. It seems especially important for men to understand this reality, because, the attributes of our physical makeup shroud the understanding from us. Also, having inherited a tradition of controlling behavior, patience is required to build trust. It is possible that within our zeal for accomplishment we have created the illusion that we have succeeded in giving our counterparts less than they deserve. However, this can only be an illusion because our counterparts do feel the lack and do prefer genuine respect when available. It would follow, that our seeming success is only a manifestation of our zeal; and, that what is really accomplished is the continuation of oppressive or controlling behavior, causing confusion and frustration for all.

It should be noted that if a man would want to have a traditionally patriarchal status within his own family, then he must assume the responsibility of teaching and maintaining moral order within his family. The level of respect which he receives from his family members, being the measure of his success. These are the differences between teaching by example, rather than by force. Between altruistic and self serving behavior. Of course, knowledge of an effective moral code would also be necessary.

A note on common respect and fearless communication. Common respect endows the reality of presence and the opportunity for sincere participation. With the understanding that decisions are the responsibility of individuals, and the impossibility of making other people's decisions for them; the patience necessary for extending this courtesy to others is achieved. This extension must take place at the behavioral level; including verbiage, only to the extent that one needs be presently aware of the actual words that one speaks at all times; whether matters are presumed simple or complicated. Further, this extension can only formulate in the realm of sincerity.

It is not unbelievable that one can be insincere with one self. Actually, what is true is that constant vigilance is required in the private of the mind to maintain sincerity; because, ideas cannot be measured or compared by physical attributes. Only through deliberation and implementation can ideas be evaluated. Naturally, As life experience is gathered, one can find that deliberation can take the place of unnecessary implementation. However, many times one can be sidetracked by one's own fantasies and imagination. What awareness provides is the ability to view the mind appropriately and to decipher between the influences that the mind is under and to choose sincerity, even at times of indulgence. This awareness can only be developed through deliberation. In interaction with others, the aware person finds that the presence of other individuals can aid the diligence required to maintain sincerity by providing ulterior perspectives. The path of salvation, although unique for every individual, is only illumined by the beloved. And so, overtime it becomes easy to discern the required degree of privacy unique to every interaction.

Fearless communication takes foundation from the understanding, that all individuals are entitled to their privacy. Sincerity does not require full disclosure; however, it does require that the rights held true for self, to be held true for others, without any degree of hypocrisy. This includes the understanding that all, including self, are entitled to their privacy. Further, sincerity requires that what is chosen to be shared, to be shared fully and honestly; even when refusing. It seems logical that, in a state of complete sincerity by all, there would be no need for aggressive behavior. Practically, what this line of thinking affords, is the understanding that the path of intimacy between two people takes form as they decide to share, what they usually hold private. The degree in which this occurs mutually, and the level of acceptance of these private matters by the respective individuals, are good indicators of the continuation or discontinuation of the relationship. On the other hand, only from a position of self respect can one recognize when he or she is being disrespected. After all, its all about mutual trust; for, in its absence, all is forsaken. Remember, honesty is the best policy. Honesty needs be chosen.

As for my testimony. It seems that every woman that I have known has somehow contributed to my learning. Some more than others. Those whom I have known intimately seem to have entered my life in perfect time, and what they left behind necessary for my development. In all of them I have found a deep desire to nurture; and, an awareness of time and change. Even in instances when the person was not aware of her intuitive side; given an environment of respect, the awareness did emerge. For my considerateness which exists objectively, I have been treated less than respectfully by many of my friends. Yet the rewards of my impartiality towards women have proven intensely satisfying. Today, I am far different in my views about the opposite sex than 1979. As such, I believe that it is not only men who seek the approval of their mothers; yet, it is the nature of people to seek the approval, and the justification for the existence, of both parents. Distinction to be made on the equality of both, instead of this seemingly unconscious inferiority complex that humanity has born towards and imposed upon women.

7. The Quagmire

The quagmire consists of three elements. The selfish, the oblivious, and the altruist. Fear is the perceived ally of the selfish; the perceived enemy of the oblivious; the altruist is never afraid. It is in this way that the oblivious is confused by the selfish. The altruist understands that in essence the fundamental necessity is to uphold the integrity of the liberty of the counterpart, and not to impose thereupon; leaving the example as the only form of real communication available. The selfish on the other hand because of the nature of insincerity needs recruit agreement to gain perceived reality. The limits of this recruitment being as wide or as subtle as the imagination will allow. It should be noted that one mind can operate in each state at different times, with respect to different issues.

Clarification needs be made that concepts such as religion, money, arms, words, etc. are intrinsically neutral. It is in their use and misuse that they are perceived to have positive or negative attributes. In this way, awareness is gained that people are ultimately judged by their intentions. The judgement however, is passed by the individual self, at the time that the decision is made. The individual's conscience is the judge. The criteria: "what if I were in my counterparts place? Would I then behave the same?"; inclusive of: The fact that most of the time the Self is the only counterpart; and, given the unchangeability of the past, and the autonomy of the memory system, that ultimately, the Self is always a counterpart as well. There in being the measure. The sentencing is between a whole or compromised conscience. The price of a compromised conscience, is relative limitation on growth, through fear. The bounty of a whole conscience, is life without fear.

Healing of a compromise is dependent on the availability of the opportunity in time. The opportunities seemingly arise spontaneously and beyond individual control; therefor, the length of time is unique in each case. The recognition of those opportunities is only available to the individual that has already made the decision and is consciously considerate of the conscience in the present. "Treat others and yourself as you would prefer to be treated."

8. Time

To put time into perspective, it is necessary to understand that time is all we really have. The things we own will all be claimed by others in time. Further, what complicates the matter is that we never know when the supply is finished.

Aside from philosophy, the indisputable facts of our reality remain to be: That one does not know how or when he or she is born; and, that one does not know how or when he or she finds his or her mate; and, that one does not know how or when he or she will die. These are non negotiable, at least within the human condition. Grace exists; because, only in this condition, the leverage required for breaking the influence of fear is available. Fear, to varying extent, seems to be a necessary, or at least a very real component of infancy; due to fragility, ignorance, and overall helplessness. Yet, the very temporary nature of the human condition, coupled with the capability of growth over time; provide the necessary criteria for salvation from fear.

Fear is the psychological counter part to the pain sensory system of the body, including the balance and the reflux systems. At this basic level fear is a very real part of the human condition. Yet, it is only at this level that the existence of actual or potential pain is precondition, to the existence of fear or concern. All other forms of fear being emanations of this psychological part of the individual, without any basis. With the inclusion of "possibilities" in the definition of "potential pain", one can find as many emanations as there are possibilities. Continued existence of these emanations over time can cause physical pain, by distracting the individual from becoming aware of the gravitational field which surrounds us.

Pain is the body's way of informing the individual that measures need be taken; or, that changes need to be made in the manner of living and thinking. As such, only in a practical sense, much of what growth is, seems to involve the overcoming of pain.

Whether one chooses a whole conscience or a compromised one, can take the same amount of effort in time, with entirely different results over time. Keeping in mind that the human condition always ends the same; and, that usually life isn't all that short after all. Compromise only seems easier at the time of the decision making; yet, over the course of the long run, a whole conscience does not require the use of the memory system in maintaining perceived integrity and, is maintained with far greater ease. Fear of death or the concept of untimely death, are ludicrous ideas to the conscience that is maintained whole. The glory that is the opportunity to live ever present.

Given the premise that time is all that we really have in this world, it follows that the only real gift that one can give to others is time, and not when it is not required. The things that are shared remain as tokens of the time spent. Leaving the criteria of requirement to the individual's choosing; again, the important factor is that what is chosen to be shared, be given without expectation of anything in return. If in the process of giving; the giver leaves the recipient with a sense of indebtedness, then what is given is not a gift at all, rather an investment. Further, to the sincere individual it is important that what is shared be whole and of value to the recipient; whether it be knowledge, information, things, etc. In this way life can become a continuous exercise in giving, for what is gathered today can be shared at appropriate times in the future. In the areas of things and private information, care should be exercised to not give away that which one wishes to keep; weather for commerce or for personal enjoyment. Because what is given is only to be given freely, and patiently. All are entitled to refuse. In the case of knowledge it is true that it cannot be given away; and, that by sharing, it only increases. Further it is true that knowledge is the most appreciated token of all.

The mysterious aspect of reality takes shape, because the conceived is born without knowledge. Further the mysterious aspect of reality exists; because, what is a mystery can only be uncovered by the understanding of the seeker. Even if divulged, it is not known until understood by the listener. In some cases, understanding can come far later than the time of listening or reading. Yet, remember that all we really have is time; and, that what requires great effort at the outset, can occur naturally if practiced over time. The information does exist; however, it will not track you down. What is necessary is to be a seeker of wisdom; and, in time you shall find, for the information is in existence. Fear is the only thing that will keep you from it. Yet remember, that the fragile state of the newborn is temporary; and, that many of our fears are carried forward within the memory of that helpless state, even if they are no longer useful. Further, the wisdom gained will serve effectively in the undoing of the very fears that will hold you back. The practice itself causes healthfulness; because, ultimately an upright mind can only be housed in an upright body. Thus, the appropriate structural geometry of the human posture can be discovered. Manifestly realizing that gravity is either a source of pressure or a source of support, in relation to the body.

9. Music

Music was always a refuge for me. The most effective by far, ever since childhood. For those who find learning enjoyable, any of the creative arts can offer excellent opportunity. However, it should be noted that after all, improvement is a function of time. Aside from effort and practice which are also necessary; the passing of time allows for the maturity of thoughts, given continued interest.

In music I found the ability to suspend conscious thought for brief periods of time. In songs I found good advice. The classics usually all contain good emotion, as well as information. Pleasantness, and whether I identify with the sentiments; seem to be my main criteria for preference. As a song writer and performer, my goal has always been to create works that will please the listener.

Now I spend my days trying to put an act together, so I can take the show on the road. Maybe I'll see you out there. To all those musicians whom have kept me

company over the years; you've been my best friends.
To God I extend praise for having so created.